Bhaskar Mili

India, Israel, and the United States in post cold war world order

GRIN Verlag

Bibliografische Information der Deutschen Nationalbibliothek:

Die Deutsche Bibliothek verzeichnet diese Publikation in der Deutschen National-
bibliografie; detaillierte bibliografische Daten sind im Internet über http://dnb.d-
nb.de/ abrufbar.

Imprint:

Copyright © 2014 GRIN Verlag GmbH
Druck und Bindung: Books on Demand GmbH, Norderstedt Germany
ISBN: 978-3-656-74092-6

This book at GRIN:

http://www.grin.com/en/e-book/279019/india-israel-and-the-united-states-in-post-
cold-war-world-order

"INDIA - ISRAEL AND THE UNITED STATES IN THE POST COLD WAR WORLD ORDER"

Total Words: 5578

Submitted by

Bhaskar Mili

Assistant professor

D.K.D.College, Dergaon, Golaghat, Assam, India

Introduction

Israel is a newly created Jewish State in the Middles-East region by the United Nations in 1948. Before its creation, the Jewish were living in Palestine as refugee and later formed the State of Israel with the help of Britain and the United States of America.

The Jewish originally belonged to Palestine, but were driven out of it by the Romans in 71AD.[1] After the World War-I, when Palestine was became a mandate of Britain, a large number of Jewish began to arrive in Palestine which was inhabited by the Arabs. These created an alarm among the Arabs for losing their land to the Jewish. The Arabs had protested against it and demanded independent Palestine for the Arabs and an end to the immigration of the Jewish. But the persecutions of Jewish in Germany after 1933 had caused a flood of refugee and by 1940 half of the populations of Palestine were Jewish.[2] In 1937, the British government had set up the Peel Commission[3] to deal with the problem which had proposed for dividing Palestine into two separate States, one for the Arabs and other for the Jewish; but the idea was totally rejected by the Arabs. In 1939, the British had tried to resolve the problem by offering an independent Arab state within ten years and an imposition of restriction on Jewish immigration to ten thousand a year; but this time Jews had rejected the proposal. After the end of the World war-II, the British were weakened by the war and felt it unable to deal with the problem and asked the United Nations to tackle this complicated issue. As a result, in November 1947, the UN had voted to divide Palestine and form an independent Jewish State. In May 1948, David Ben Gurion declared the independence of the new state of Israel[4]. The new State was immediately attacked by Egypt, Syria, Jordan, Iraq and Lebanon.[5] Since its creation, Israel has continuously involved in direct or indirect war with the Arab States. With the creation of the State of Israel, the Middle-East became a battle ground between Israel and other States in the region.

India and Israel have a very short diplomatic history. Though India had recognized Israel as an independent State in 1950[6], but had not established any diplomatic relation with it. Due to certain internal as well as external circumstances India maintains a distance from Israel. India, after her independence in 1947, required necessary funds and technological helps from both the blocs (US led bloc and USSR led bloc) for her economic and industrial development. On the other hand, Israel after being established had joined the bloc politics by becoming a member of the US led bloc. At the same time India followed the policy of non-alignment, which is against the participation of any bloc politics. At this juncture, India has been maintaining a very good relationship with the Arab world on which she is dependent for her energy requirement and a large numbers of Indian workers have been working in these Arab States which are also a source of earning for foreign exchange. The presence of a large number of Muslim populations in India and the fear of being criticized by Pakistan to be a partisan with the Zionist State, India decided not to maintain any diplomatic relations with the Jewish state.

But the situation was changed after the end of the Gulf War in 1991, when Israel emerged as a dominant power in the Middle-East region. On the other hand, the end of Cold War had also changed the world scenario, which forced India to re-orient her foreign policy. Since most of the armaments of Indian forces were supplied by the former Soviet Union, the disintegration of the Soviet Union caused a serious problem for the supply of armament to Indian military forces. In such situation India needed an alternative reliable supplier of arms for her forces. During that period it was the United States of America or Israel who could replace the position of the former Soviet Union. But India's relations with the United States was not smooth due to their differences in the era of Cold War and America's close ties with Pakistan, so India left only with one option i.e. Israel with whom India has no diplomatic relations. On the other hand, Israel has a very close relationship with the US. The US had used her veto power in the UN for as much as 32 times in support of Israel[7]. Besides most of the weapons that Israel could supply to India needs prior American permission due to joint productions by the two States. After the disintegration of the Soviet Union, India lost the support of Super Power on her international issues. To secure the support of the sole Super Power, i.e. the United States of America, India decided to establish diplomatic relations with Israel to give a signal to Washington regarding India's intention to redesign her foreign policy in the post Cold war environment. It is interesting to note that despite having good relations with the Arab countries, the Arab League never supported India on Kashmir issue, instead in all occasions it had supported Pakistani claim over it. After the conclusion of Camp David Treaty between Israel and Egypt in 1978[8], some of the Arab States started establishing diplomatic relations with the State of Israel, which also helped India to change her decision regarding Israel. On the whole, India was interested to be a part of the ongoing West Asian Peace process, for which the United States of America and Israel put a condition upon India to establish full diplomatic relations with Israel to become a party to the peace process. According to Yegar, the Deputy Director General of the Israeli MFA, at that time stressed that participation in the Madrid Peace Conference[9] had become a matter of prestige for India. However the Government of Israel made it quite clear that countries that refused to have normal diplomatic relations with her and having such relations with the Arab countries, would be barred from the Madrid Conference.[10] The Indian Government realised the sensitivity of the moment and finally made the decision to establish diplomatic relations with Israel. On 23rd January 1992, then Foreign Secretary of

India J.N. Dixit, was authorized to announce India's decision to formally established bilateral relations. On 23rd January 1992, Dixit had discussed with the senior cabinet ministers regarding the timing of the establishment of diplomatic relations with Israel. In his memoirs Dixit stated,

"I was authorized to make a formal announcement of India's decision to establish diplomatic relations with Israel and the opening of embassies in each other's capitals. I made this announcement on 24 January".[11]

Though the Government of India was trying to postpone the decision on diplomatic relations with Israel, but due to firm Israeli stance and certain fine-tuning elements finally forced India to make her decision.

The three key factors were instrumental in influencing the timing of the Indian transformation of foreign policy towards Israel at the focal point of the change process. These three change determinants were:

1) The establishment of diplomatic relations between China and Israel on 24 January 1992.

2) The opening of the third round of the Middle East peace talks in Moscow, which took place between 28 and 29 January 1992.

3) The official visit of Prime Minister Narasimha Rao to the US, to attend the UN Security Council meeting in New York, which took place at the beginning of February 1991.

P. R. Kumaraswamy, Professor at the School of International Studies, Jawaharlal Nehru University (JNU), New Delhi and a specialist on Indo-Israel relations stated: *"Since 1947, Washington had been nudging India to modify its policy toward Israel. It was not accidental that normalization was announced on the eve of Rao's visit to New York."*[12]

An official announcement making the establishment of fully-fledged diplomatic relations between India and Israel, was published simultaneously in Jerusalem, New Delhi and Moscow (where the Israeli Minister of Foreign Affairs was on an official visit participating in the third round of the peace talks) on 29 January 1992. On the same day, the Secretary of the Ministry of External Affairs of India sent a letter to the Israeli Consul in Bombay, Giora Becher, informing him of the following Indian announcement:

"The governments of India and Israel have decided to establish full diplomatic relations. Embassies will be opened in Tel Aviv and New Delhi. Modalities regarding this arrangement will be worked out through normal diplomatic channels. In pursuance of the above, I have been directed to invite your government to open an embassy in New Delhi."[13]

Some of the Arab states were opposed to India's closer relationship with the State of Israel. According to P.R. Kumaraswamy, *"Contrary to past fears and apprehensions, the newly established relations with Israel did not inhibit India from pursuing productive relations with a number of Middle Eastern countries."*[14] While J.N. Dixit was instructed by Prime Minister Rao to brief the Muslim countries in detail about the decision to establish diplomatic relations with Israel and also to instruct the Indian Ambassadors in Arab and other Islamic countries to brief the respective governments to which they were accredited. In his memories, Dixit stated;

"Some of the Arab Ambassadors were aggressively resentful when a couple of my ambassadorial colleagues crossed thresholds of political courtesy and mentioned that India would face uncertain consequences, I decided to take the bull by the horns…I declared that India had not received any reciprocity on the Kashmir issue despite our longstanding support to several Islamic countries in international fora (arena). I also underlined the fact that India would not accept any extraneous limitations on its sovereign right of determining its policy decisions within the framework of Indian interests. There was some criticism of India in the Arab media. Some questioned the wisdom of India's decision. But this decision did not affect Indo-Arab relations negatively."[15]

India's new foreign policy towards the Middle-East had marked a paradigm shift from an ideological approach to a pragmatic one and preferred to deal with secular republic of Israel rather than conservative Sheikhdoms. India had changed her stands from one sided position in Arab- Israel conflict to a balanced one. Since independence India has been maintaining cordial relationships with the Middle-East and Arabian Muslim countries, but they used to have a pro-Pakistani attitude in their policies. India had been invited to attend the summit of Islamic states at Rabat (Morocco) in 1969, but due to protests and threat from Pakistan of their withdrawal from the summit, India's invitation to the summit was cancelled. Again when the Organization of Islamic Conferences (OIC) was founded in 1971 had traditionally been critical of India's international politics in particular with respect to Kashmir as the Muslim countries allowed their citizens to fight in Kashmir as part of a pan-Islamic jihadist movement.[16]

In 1991, conference of the Foreign Ministers of the OIC, in Karachi, set up a fact finding mission and proposed that it would be sent to Jammu and Kashmir in order to report on the situation there. Following India's refusal to allow the mission into the country, the OIC summit condemned India for its violation of human rights in Jammu and Kashmir, thereby encouraging Pakistan to pursue an active Islamic anti-Indian foreign policy. Despite India's pro-Muslim and pro-Arab foreign policy, the OIC consistently supported Pakistan against India over the Kashmir issue. Finally in 1991, India realised the importance of diplomatic relations with Israel as a counter move against the Arab and Muslim world. Due to such reasons, at the beginning of the nineties, India started reconsidering her relation with the radical Arab world and democratic Israel. With the backdrop of changing geo-political situation in West Asia as well as the changing strategic perception, India now finally began to redirect her diplomatic tools.

The attempts to normalize the bilateral relationship with Israel were started during the terms of Janata Party Government in 1977. The then Israeli Foreign Minister, Moshe Dayan made a secret visit to New Delhi to meet the Indian Prime Minister Moraji Desai[17], but not much came out of that visit. The contacts resumed towards the end of Indira Gandhi's second innings. But the process was referred only as technical cooperation by the official's familiar with the back ground. Later on Rajiv

Gandhi carried forward the process of ties between India and Israel. But he was not taking any grand initiative due to the possible reactions of the Muslim population within India. The ground works for normalization of the relations were prepared during 1990-91 when India supported to revoke the UN resolution of 1975 of equating Zionism with Racism[18]. Finally it was P. V. Narasimha Rao's government that recognized the changing geo-political scenario and moved quickly to normalize relations between the two states. J.N. Dixit, the former Foreign Secretary of India, in his memoirs stated that:

"The Prime Minister, in a number of internal meetings, highlighted a significant and relevant precondition to our taking this policy decision. He said that he would first take senior members of his own party into confidence about the rationale of establishing relations with Israel. He observed that after ensuring a consensus in domestic and political terms, he would hold discussions with Yasser Arafat to gauge his reaction and only then finalize the decision".[19]

Being an emerging power, India wants to do business with the Middle East region as whole; therefore it wants to maintain good relations with all states of the region whether it is Israel or the Arab World. Because of such changing situations and requirements, former Prime Minister, Narasimha Rao, had decided to establish diplomatic relationship and finally in January 1992, both India and Israel had established full diplomatic relations. The normalization of relations left both countries have to explore many areas and they rapidly involved in these areas. Since then, the two sides have a broad range of cooperation in different areas ranging from agriculture, water management technique, use of solar energy, science & technology and in defense sector. Despite the development of a good relationship and cooperation on different sectors, India's stands on Palestine issue are still playing an obstacle to develop a warmer relationship with Israel. Shortly before the establishment of the diplomatic relations with Israel, in January 1992 the PLO leader Yasir Arafat visited India to discuss about India's decision to normalize her relations with Israel. In his statement, the PLO leader stated that the exchange of ambassadors and the mutual recognition are acts of exercising Indian sovereignty and there should not be an adverse reaction by the Arabs on this matter.

It is being observed that the relevant fundamental national interests and strategic goals of the two nations were taken into consideration by the formulators of foreign policy in terms of micro international politics and diplomacy and influenced in the changing process of foreign policy. Such formative determinants of the Indian foreign policy transformation towards Israel were the end of the Cold War and the collapse of the Soviet Union. It also signified the end of the bipolar world as well as the Cold War had made tremendous changes to Indian foreign policy.

The collapse of the Soviet Union along with the paradigm of a stable new political world also meant that the concept of nonalignment had no validity. In the new era of uni-polarity, India could change its foreign policy towards Israel and Prime Minister Rao could rectify the anomalous situation, which had existed for over four decades between the two countries. Earlier, India's Israel policy had coincided with Cold War politics, and Israel's identification with the West had provided an ideological basis for India's pro-Arab orientation.[20] In short the collapse of the Soviet Union and the emergence of the US as the sole superpower, the momentum for the peace process in the Middle East and the commonality of problems between the two states were some of the factors that caused the shift in India's stance towards Israel. The fundamental changes in international environments, strategic interest and influence of generating determinants help in shifting Indian foreign policy towards Israel. J.N. Dixit have the opinion that the foregoing developments, a fundamental re-examination of India's relations with Israel became pertinent in the post-Gulf War international situation; India considered it suitable to establish diplomatic relations with Israel and to initiate bilateral cooperation across the board with that country.[21] While reviewing the Indian foreign policy towards Israel, Dixit states that the geo-strategic interests of India carried a great deal in the normalization of relations with Israel.

India was concerned about the emergence of Islamic fundamentalist elements in Afghanistan, Saudi Arabia and Iran to Central Asia and spreading from there to Kashmir. Both India and Israel feared the rise of Islamic fundamentalism in Central Asia and were concerned that the Central Asian republics might fall prey to Islamic fundamentalism after the disintegration of the Soviet Union. India was particularly concerned that possible regional disorder in the region might break out because of widespread violence. As such both India and Israel wanted a reduction of Islamic fundamentalist elements in the entire region.

It has been observed that, during the tenure of the Bharatiya Janata Party (BJP) led National Democratic Alliance (NDA) government, the Indo-Israel relation had witness a new height of development. During this period, numbers of agreements were signed between the two States on socio- economic, art & culture, science & technology, trade and commerce and on security related matters. There were numbers of important bilateral visits taken place during the NDA regime. The visit of Home Minister, L. K. Advani and External Affairs Minister, Jaswant Singh in June 2000 were the highest level visit made by any Indian leaders since the normalization of relations in 1992.The visit had initiated the process of strategic cooperation between the two States. The visit of Israeli Prime Minister Arial Sharon in 2003 was one of the most important developments of the bilateral relation. Till the visit of Sharon, the Indo-Israel relations was accorded as a low profile in international relations, but India's decision to give a red carpet welcome to Sharon in 2003, had drawn the attention of the different sections of international community. After Soviet Union, now Israel becomes one of the main suppliers of military equipments to India. Within this short diplomatic relationship, both the states had signed numbers of agreements of cooperation in different areas and issued joint statements to fight against global terrorism. There were numbers of exchange of visits from either side to increase cooperation in all aspects. The visit of Ezar Weizmann, the President of Israel, in 1996-1997 to India was the first highest level visit from Israel[22], helps the two states to cooperate each other on numbers of areas including agriculture, culture, tourism and defense. During his visit, the President inaugurated numbers of agriculture related joint projects in India and also offered to sell Barak-I missile defense systems and other military equipments to India. Shimon Peres, President of Israel had visited India for four times to strengthen the relationships and was the first Israeli Minister to visit India after normalization of relation in 1992. From Indian side several Chief Ministers of different states, senior defense officials, Chief of Arms Forces, numbers of Central Ministers, scientist and military personnel, have visited Israel to increase mutual cooperation on different areas. But it was only during the BJP government that highest levels of bilateral contact were taken place between the two States. The most interesting fact is that, like the BJP, the Likud party in Israel is known for its hard-line views, and promoted the idea of *"Akhand Bharat"* and *"Greater Israel"* respectively.[23]

Subsequently, the visit of Prime Minister Arial Sharon to India in September, 2003 had further strengthened the relationship. During this period, both the states had concluded a significant numbers of military treaties, on the basis of which India has been acquiring advance Phalcon airborne warning and control system and other military equipments from Israel. Both the states are more reticent about their military cooperation. But after the Kargil conflict in 1999, the military cooperation between the two States becomes public. By 2002, Israel's non- military trade with India had grown to more than six times what it used to be in 1992, i.e. US $1.27 billion as compared to US $ 202 million[24]. Regardless of how much non-military ties have expanded between the States, Israel is India's second largest seller of armament after Russia. On the other hand, India is Israel's second largest trading partner in Asia after China.

Role of the United States of America

The US and the American Jewish Community plays an important role in the normalization and development of the Indo-Israel relations. In the early part of the 90s decade, the Indian economy was at the stage of moribund condition and to revive the economy India needed funds from the World Bank and the IMF. The US has the control over these financial institutions on the matter regarding sanction of grants and loans. The differences between India and the US during the era of Cold war created problems in the way of securing American support to get financial assistances from the WB and IMF. The non-establishment of diplomatic relations with Israel, to some extent had dissatisfied the US towards India. Finally in January 1992, India had established diplomatic relationship with the State of Israel. The establishment of diplomatic relation with Israel was a move by India to come closer to the US and secure its support for the redevelopment of Indian economy. Finally, it was due to economic assistances from the IMF and World Bank that India had able to re-structure her economy.

After the disintegration of the Soviet Union in early 1990s, India lost the supplier of weapons for her forces and the US and Israel was the only available alternatives who could supply weapons for Indian forces. On the other hand, a close military ties with Pakistan prevented the US to supply the same to India and in such situation Israel remained as the only alternative that could fulfill India's requirements. But most of the military technologies developed by Israel are funded by the US, so it required the approval of the US before selling or transferring these technologies to India. Therefore, India needed to develop her relationships with the US to secure permissions to get weapons and military technologies from Israel. It was only after the clearance from the US that Israel able to deliver three Phalcon early warning radar (AWACS) systems to India; that was earlier denied to China due to opposition from the US. Again, due to the opposition from the US, India and Israel was not able to proceed on the agreement on Arrow missile systems. The sale of huge numbers of Israeli weapons and technologies to India are possible only due to the approval from the US that successively helped Israel to emerge as the number one supplier of arms to India. Within a very short period the Indian military purchases from Israel crossed the mark of US $10 billion. By the end of 2006, Israel surpassed Russia as the main supplier of weapons to India in terms of annual military transactions.

The development of bilateral relations between India and Israel is also helped in the development of Indo-US relations. After the disintegration of the former Soviet Union, India lost the support of super power on her different international matters and to secure the support of the sole super power, India decided to move through Israel to secure the US support. As such simultaneously, India needs to develop her relations with both Israel and the US to secure her national interest. To some extent, the establishment of diplomatic relations with Israel and the liberalization of Indian economy in 1992 helped in this regard. The first helped in the development of relations with Israel, whereas the second helped to develop relations with the US. After the liberalization of the Indian economy, the US was attracted to the large Indian consumer markets and to fulfill its own economic interests, the US too came forward to develop relations with India. Besides, after the disintegration of Soviet Union and end of Cold war, the differences of the cold war era were subsided by the two sides and the development of a closer relationship between China and Pakistan became a matter of concerned for the both states.

The emergence of Peoples' Republic of China as challenge to the US hegemony became a matter of concerned for the US to protect its interests in the region and to maintain balance of power in the South Asian region the US started developing strategic cooperation with India and started arming India to check Chinese expansion. The direct supply of weapons from the US to India could provoke China to develop closer strategic relationship with Pakistan; which is not a good sign for the US interests. In such situation the US decided to supply advance weapons technologies to India through indirect channel, i.e. via Israel. Again as a sign of cooperation, in June 2009, despite Chinese opposition, the US provided diplomatic help to India to get US $2.9 billion loan from the <u>Asian Development Bank</u>.

A coalition of the US-India Political Action Committee (USINPAC), America- Israel Political Action Committee (AIPAC) and American Jewish Committee (AJC) has extensively lobbied to secure permission from the US to allow Israel to sell three Phalcon early warning radar systems of worth US $ 1.1 billion to India. Finally in 2004, the US had approved the sale of three Israeli Phalcon Airborne Warning and Control Systems to India that Washington previously prevented Tel Aviv from selling to China in 1998. The US administration was worried about the Phalcons supplied to India, that could impact the balance between India and Pakistan, but the concerns were evaporated in the warmth of the India-US-Israel strategic relationship. The Phalcon early-warning systems would give India the capability to look nearly 200 kilometers inside Pakistan territory and make it difficult for Pakistani troops and war planes to move without being detected. The Phalcon system acts as a major force multiplier which would drastically alter the military balance in South Asia. In the recent time both Indian and Israeli lobbies are lobbing at US for a clearance on the sale of Arrow missile defense system to Delhi. The Arrow deal could significantly shift the Asian balance of power in favour of India, as it would make the country less vulnerable to attacks from Pakistan or China. The Indian-American lobby and the Jewish American lobby in the US have teamed up to persuade the administration to clear the sale. The Jewish-Indian alliance in the US has combined forces on electoral politics in order to defeat those whom they perceive as antagonistic to both Israel and India. The lobbies of two countries are working together on a number of domestic and foreign affairs issues, such as hatred, crimes, immigration, anti-terrorism legislation and backing pro-Israel and pro-India candidates. It was due to the efforts of these two powerful groups that pro-Pakistan, anti-India and anti-Israel Congresswoman Cynthia McKinney was defeated in the congressional election.

The influential American Jewish community and the Jewish lobby in the US helped in the building of close economic relations with the US. The American Jewish Lobby received special attention from Prime Minister Narasimha Rao in 1991 when the Indian government applied to the World Bank and the International Monetary Fund (IMF) for urgent support. Rao realised that the Jewish Lobby in US could be instrumental or an obstacle in such request, as it had proved to be four years earlier. In May 1987, after the Israeli tennis players were not allowed to participate in the Davis Cup tournament in New Delhi, following an Anti Defamation league protest, the American Congress support was reduced from US $ 60 million to US$ 35 million. In fact, India was subsequently forced to allow the Israeli players to take part in the tournament. In 1991, Prime Minister Rao realised the necessity to utilize the political weight of the American Jewish organisations in favour of India when the country was on the verge of economic collapse.

Noted Pakistani strategic expert, Mohammed Ali Khan describes the potential contribution of the American Jewish organisations to India: *"Normal relations with Israel could help turn pro-Israeli lobbies in the US to show at least a modicum of leaning towards India."*[25]

The September 11, 2001 terrorist attack on the US had changed the entire political and strategical equations. The post 9/11 situations helped in the development of strategic alliance between India and Israel. In his address to a gathering of American Jewish in 2003, India's National Security Advisor Brajesh Mishra, proposed for the development of Indo-Israel-US tripartite alliances to fight against global terrorism. In his address, Mishra told that the democratic States like India, Israel and the US are the primary targets of terrorists, so they should form a viable alliance to fight against them. In their war against terrorism, the US had allowed Israel to channelize high technologies to India. In

2010, the US and India had started the process of strategic dialogues between the two states which is a sign of greater partnership on security matters.

The growing Indo-Israel alliance is also strengthening the US strategic designs for the region. India holds a significant place in the September 20, 2002 National Security Strategy of the US. Like Israel in West Asia, the US needed close ally in South Asia to confront terrorists in Afghanistan and Pakistan as well as to overcome the challenges posed by China. To mark the growing Indo-US strategic relationship, both the states had concluded the Indo-US civil nuclear deal in 2008. Meanwhile the Jewish lobby in the American Congress had played a significant role to go through the deal. According to Robert D Blackwill, the US ambassador to India,

"The United States has undertaken a transformation in its bilateral relationship with India. We are the two largest democracies. We share an interest in fighting terrorism and in creating a strategically stable Asia. We start with a view of India as a growing world power with which we have common strategic interests." One of his articles published in The Hindu, Blackwill wrote,

"Taken together our defense cooperation and military sales activities intensify the working relationships between the respective armed forces, build mutual military capacities for future joint operations and strengthen Indian military capability, which is in America's interest."

He also wrote, *"An Indian military that is capable of operating effectively alongside its American counterparts remains an important goal of our bilateral defense relationship. What we have achieved since January 2001 builds a strong foundation on which to consummate this strategic objective, which will promote peace and freedom in Asia and beyond."*

The views of the outgoing American ambassador clearly highlight the height of Indo-US relations in the post 9/11 attack. In the development of the relation, the American Jewish Community has played an important role by their continuous lobby for greater Indo-Israel –US cooperation.

---

[1] R.S. Chaurasia (2005), *History of Middle East*, New Delhi: Atlantic Publishers and Distributors (P) Ltd. P.95.

[2] P. Bassler Gerhard (1997), Attempts to Settle Jewish Refugees in Newfoundland and Labrador, 1934-1939, *Annual 5, Chapter 7, The Simon Wiesenthal Center*, Los Angeles, California, p.2.

[3] The Peel Commission Report July 1937, pp.2-13.

[4] "Independence Day 1948: The Most Crowded Hours in... History", (editorial) *The Historma*, Tel Aviv, p.2.

[5] Official documents on '1948 Arab-Israel War', *US Department of State, Office of the Historian,*US: p.1-2

[6] Mezard Isabelle Saint (2010), India and Israel: an unlikely alliance, *Le Monde Diplomatique*, Paris: p.1.

[7] Neff Donald (1993), 'U.S. Vetoes of U.N. Resolutions on Behalf of Israel', *Washington Report Sept/Oct 1993*, p. 82.

[8] Document published on 'Camp David Accords' by Israeli Ministry of Foreign Affairs, pp.3-4.

[9] **The Madrid Conference of 1991** was a peace conference held from 30 October to 1 November 1991 in Madrid, hosted by Spain and co-sponsored by the United States and the Soviet Union. It was an attempt by the

international community to revive the Israeli–Palestinian peace process through negotiations, involving Israel and the Palestinians as well as the Arab countries, including Jordan, Lebanon and Syria.

[10] Itzhak Gerberg, (2008), *The Changing Nature of Israeli-Indian Relations: 1948-2005*, South Africa: University of South Africa, P.298.

[11] J.N. Dixit (1996), *My South Block years : Memoirs of a foreign secretary,* New Delhi: UBS Publishers' Distributors, 1st edition, p.312.

[12] P.R. Kumaraswamy (2002), 'India- Israel relations: Humble beginnings, a bright future', (editorial), Washington:*The American Jewish Committee*, p.4.

[13] Itzhak Gerberg (2008), op.cit. P. 343.

[14] P.R. Kumaraswamy (2010), *India's Israel Policy*, Columbia University Press, p.352.

[15] J.N. Dixit (1996), op.cit. p.312-313

[16] Stephen P. Cohen (2001), *India – Emerging Power*, Washington DC: Brookings Institution Press, p.248.

[17] Verinder Grover (1984), *West Asia and India's Foreign Policy,* New Delhi: Deep & Deep Publication, P. 170.

[18] Aftab Kamal Pasha (2002), *Arab-Israeli Peace Process An Indian Perspective*, New Delhi: Manas Publication, p.69.

[19] J.N.Dixit (1996), op.cit. p. 311.

[20] P.R Kumaraswamy (2002), 'India and Israel: emerging partnership', *Journal of Strategic Studies*, Frank Cass: Vol 25, issue 4. pp. 205- 207.

[21] Dixit J.N. (1996), op.cit. pp. 309- 310.

[22] Timeline of Indo-Israel Relations (editorial),*The Israel Project,* Jerusalem: p.1.

[23] Praful Adagale (2012), 'India And Israel Strategic Partnership: Challenges And Opportunities' – Analysis, *Eurasia Review News and Analysis,* p.2.

[24] Mahwish Hafee (2009), 'India- Israel relations', *Asianet*, Pakistan: p.6.

[25] Itzhak Gerberg (2010), 'India-Israel bilateral relations in the international system', *India-Israel Relations Strategic Interests, Politics and Diplomatic Pragmatism,* Haifa: Israel Defense College, p.24.